Honey and Poison

Pedro Tamen's Portuguese publications include:

Poems for Every Day
Blood, Water and Wine
Lapinova's First Book
Poems to This
Daniel in the Lion's Den
Written from Memory
Forty-Two Sonnets
Now, To Be
The Circulatory System
Horace and Coriace
Within Moments
Delphus, Opus 12
Previously Unpublished Works
After Seeing
The Pennant of Charon
Unspeakable Memory

Also by Richard Zimler

Translations:

The Secret Life of Images by Al Berto

Novels:

Unholy Ghosts
The Last Kabbalist of Lisbon
The Angelic Darkness

PEDRO TAMEN

Honey and Poison

translated from the Portuguese
by
Richard Zimler

CARCANET

INSTITUTO PORTUGUÊS DO LIVRO E DAS BIBLIOTECAS

MINISTÉRIO DOS NEGÓCIOS ESTRANGEIROS INSTITUTO CAMÕES

MINISTÉRIO DA CULTURA

Translator's Acknowledgements

Grateful thanks to Pedro Tamen for his patience in answering so many questions. Thanks, as well, to Michael Collins and Portugal 600.

INSTITUTO CAMÕES   INSTITUTO PORTUGUÊS DO LIVRO E DAS BIBLIOTECAS   MINISTÉRIO DA CULTURA

First published in Great Britain in 2001 by
Carcanet Press Limited
4th Floor, Conavon Court
12–16 Blackfriars Street
Manchester M3 5BQ

A CIP catalogue record for this book
is available from the British Library

ISBN 1 85754 540 0

The publisher acknowledges financial assistance
from the Arts Council of England

Set in Monotype Garamond by XL Publishing Services, Tiverton
Printed and bound in England by SRP Ltd, Exeter

Contents

from *WRITTEN FROM MEMORY* (1973)

from *FORTY-TWO SONNETS* (1973)

from *NOW, TO BE* (1975)

from *THE CIRCULATORY SYSTEM* (1978)

from *PREVIOUSLY UNPUBLISHED WORKS* (1965–1991)

from *Poems for Every Day* (1956)

'Green time of poplars and willows and rivers unknowing, and of gentle banks...'

Green time of poplars and willows and rivers unknowing, and of
gentle banks...
My thirst was with yours, wrapped in shadows along the shores.
And there was nothing more child-like or more coupled than our
simple and pure permanence.
The gods were dead; now there was only one, bellowing his blood
into dry veins,
and sending out young birds, like ornamentation, into the solid
harmony of your body.
The cicadas were singing and it wasn't day, the skies were
unendingly blue,
and there were springs for us, and cool fresh soil... Who can know
– or does know – how to offer thanks?
A single moment was our dawn and in that silence everything was
revealed to us.
Imperfect, humble, and peaceful, our science was being in our place.

'At that time living was the best thing in the world'

At that time living was the best thing in the world.
When the sun rose the people would all gaze around,
and men were living as children beyond the hills.
It was a plain, wide, as all plains must by necessity be,
and flat because everything was a certainty.
At that time we had just been created and were just like the grasses
and flowers.

You,
so perfect that it was impossible for you not to be,
and so uplifted, like a swallow's laughter,
you were by my side, fresh of nature,
and there were neither motives nor reasons because we knew
everything.
Our theology was the kiss of the closest child
and our easing down into the earth like leaves of the same plant,
grateful, compact, conscious.
Looking up, the sky was opening and all the Angels were coming to
sit at the edge
and were giggling with laughter just like us.
I was singing songs more beautiful than those without words.
and you were listening to me in silence and with eyes wide-open,
exactly as you would
listen to all of the other sounds around us.

'Time'

Time,
lengthy, beautiful, arid, peaceful,
time without memory,
our eyes in flight.

Light,
light inevitable, white, consecrated.
Presence extended
breathing the high bright air.

Tears,
like the rain, the sea, the great shadows,
rivers of happiness without sense,
and certain birds.

Here is what the dogs made: detritus. Let us lift our feet
carefully. Let us listen to the long day at its centre,
the avenues that cross, the curious people,
the last form of sensation permitted by our vices. It's never worth
smiling as if it was only that unknown old man who had died.

Tomorrow, yes,

tomorrow the curtain will be raised and never again
shall it be necessary for us to avoid panicking. It was a fire, it was.
'Now wait a minute,' observed meekness, 'that's for us to judge,
for all of us to judge.'
        In the end, long shapes that stretch,
rivers of water, so pure, divided into skies – because it's true
that only in clouds, water. A great-aunt who still doesn't wear glasses
had perfect eyesight, even saw a cell.
When will we go get the luggage? When will the doorman come up?
Will we one day know how to build our cubicles? Questions wise
and blushing, the sun passed over them and they gathered in
the bright aridity. Between the head and guts
nothing was permitted to remain unpunished: Caesar,
my old friend, why, why was that?
Let us bow and lower our heads, but raise our feet.

And in the meantime, let us also swing our arms, refuse to idly bite

our nails,

put our hearts in an accompanied place,
for we are going to have to sweat. And, only in the end, water.

from *Blood, Water, and Wine* (1958)

'Now the hills descend at their ease in endless footpaths'

Now the hills descend at their ease in endless footpaths,
to the river, to the sea, to the city. And, gently, from out of the gorse,
rise the perfumes, the incense, the crowds of blazing stars.
Now flows down the blood under the offerings, now comes
its more vigorous and enclosing embrace, overwhelming everything.
Here now, Father, here is the blood of Man, the blood of the Son,
here is what spills and runs down the streets,
coming from the hills,
sluicing into the cellars.

And never again shall we forget that liquid, never again!
Here is what entered our arms and what swells our bodies,
here is what it comes to be, coursing inside in an unending river
from which we never again shall drink, hiding inside us and
                                                    connecting
things of which we are not aware, blood too great for limits.

'Excuse me, dear Lady, but why do you mourn'

Excuse me, dear Lady, but why do you mourn,
what loved one is no longer living, no longer living?
Alive and blessed will always be the fruit that is born
of the fruit-womb that was the God who has given.

'With true calm we slowly sweep away the air'

With true calm we slowly sweep away the air
and, seated, we offer our reasons. Meanwhile,
it is time itself that is slipping away
through the doors at our temples – the metallic weapons
in the eyes of children have blinded us.
The clairvoyant rose, the fleeting flora
that fills that table of ours set with another kind of hunger –
of it, we are almost ashamed, children,
almost ashamed, dear children. Today,
like tomorrow, we have our reasons and you smile,
and your slumber is our slumber, blade of the same sword
slashing the same face, on which the acids burn
under waters that are one, that timidly
consent to it, washing over eyes closed tight.

'What runs now through the grass, has in its very footprints'

What runs now through the grass, has in its very footprints,
its own reward, and to itself payment shall return one day.
Whether in breathing blowing, or flowing in winged mists,
the breeze that is born of itself becomes our pay.

An innocent hand there prepares itself another hand
inside the space that it inhabits. In the blinking of an eyelid,
all sure happiness and hurts befallen. And in the land,
fertile, the eternal earth to our feet is wed.

from *Lapinova's First Book* (1960)

'From out of you the chalice is raising'

From out of you the chalice is raising
into the air the blood of the Lord;
that is how I understand, my beloved,
that the morning has been reborn and is a blessing.

From out of you the night makes up for
the hours that I waited for good slumber.
And now each star has its master
There precisely where you are.

From out of you comes a glance nodding
toward the place of serenity where I offer again
the new days that are giving up their very being.

From you I know who it was who brought in
each minute of today, and how, remaining
placid and well placed, the night ceded to morn.

'And now – your skin'

And now – your skin.
I look again – how gentle is the swaying sea.
And I sense that the wind races and that it pins
against your body memories of moon-made luminosity.

I grow calm – your hair.
I yield – it is already morn.
The branches are serene, and upon seeing them there
in the concave of your hand the sun is born.

'The foot of night stands on its feet'

The foot of night stands on its feet
at the centre, in the heart of this hand;
let the day race past, never again
will there pass your shoulders or any wall.

Love, if I know anything, we know that made
from nothing is the wound
and even the sword's blade.

from *Poems to This* (1962)

'On ne badine pas avec l'amour'

On ne badine pas avec l'amour

Rose, solar or white of hue?
Carnation, of earth and scarlet.
Instead of nightingale, let us say owlet.
River, this is how I halt you.

'I shall not speak'

I shall not speak about this the substance, the mist
of an unsure spaceship the white-suited horseman,
nor shall I speak of this the trout that slips away
smirking out of wharves and airports.

I shall not speak of this the green of the season,
and the written bombs sheltered on bookshelves,
the bonze yellow of this square
hidden behind the savoured cinnamon of the heart.

Not of the massive unrepentant hunger,
of the fright gobbled up with beans,
of the crippled lightning bugs, hidden
in the blank paper diary.

I shall never speak of the quivering seabass –
of silver, salt and water – that is being suckled,
and of the oven near to which the girl
keeps sharpening her legs in preparation.

I shall not speak of José's bludgeon
and the bludgeonings given José throughout the morning,
I shall not speak of this the floor and the night-time hand
that digs within the silence of the mole.

My own wind runs off with the rain and keeps
going till it itself becomes mud and the space
between the simple hand and the untouched knocker.

Soccer Days

With time running out
the rose catches fire
but doesn't burn.
Unrepenting, the moonlight
becomes our looking glass and our place.
A perfect girl finished only up to
her traitorous knees chases round and round.
(Hark, the sweet glowing sky
sliding toward our breast!)

A panting tongue sets in
on soccer days.

'The hidden things in which we've erred'

The hidden things in which we've erred,
like the hidden things we've correctly done,
beloved,
and now come open.

Finale

Enlightened, say it, but missing:
no one else but we whom death has hurled
to the mercy of heavens and these waves unfurled,
where meanings are gained or go a-wanting

Now we search the seas and seabed
for the new America that lies deepest down,
for the world's very ground,
for the land our naked feet long to tread.

Either this or solitude or even a gate
very firmly locked, until there comes to us a single fish.
In contemplation we remain until a voice grants us our wish –
of dousing the still-life with a fresh coat of paint

– and risking everything in secret, like madmen
who no longer own anything keep rowing,
and continue gambling,
on the luck of being one of the chosen.

from *Daniel in the Lion's Den* (1970)

'Already past late and before too soon'

Already past late and before too soon:
like what's coming by plane from Tokyo,
for a patient that's already died,
(who is safe now, you might say)
and within the airport already lost or expired,
doesn't ever reach that leg in pain or that affliction
aching for an injection.

– that drop of yellow glass
within which shelters a wine grown speechless
that comes to transport the air from the equatorial plain,
the exhaust and discord,
reaching only this-that side of pain
and, more even than untried,
is forgotten.

'I say of you empty shells – not hollow'

I say of you empty shells – not hollow,
but huge, pregnant, inhabited.
Gazing at your hand just now
I catch a glimpse of gods near you seated.
I say of you words formed with lips,
I say of you vowels made with my very tips.

I speak, walking onward: the starry crossing
that gives us home, where days are passed,
is unique yet ever the same; even while varying,
it is always what carries us to and fro, reveals us at last,
and in Grace gives us grounding.

Open your arms, urgent and unconstrained,
it is not only me whom you hold;
you shelter languid lights, vigorous winds,
distant calms, shores, slime, snow…
Shells are just like this: when we enfold
them in our hands, serrated, singing away,
who can know whether it is they we hold
today, tomorrow, or yesterday?

'Air currents are rippling'

Air currents are rippling
the minimal movements
of the rabbits kissing
with eyes wide open.

And so we send
the sun into night
living then
in the shadows of the sea.

'The sea is far away, but it is we who are its wind'

The sea is far away, but it is we who are its wind;
and the remembrance that it brings, to become the sea,
is the memory of itself and another, and of the air of your mouth
where the silence grazes and the night accepts.
Where are you, what mist disquiets me
more than not seeing the eyes of the morning
with which you yourself see it and give assent?
Hair, fingers, salt and the elongated skin,
where they hide what your life gives them;
and it's with solemn hands, fleeting,
that I gather you up alive and concede to myself
the hour in which the waves grow indistinct
and nothing becomes necessary beside the sea.

'I talk. I speak to you of blues and greens'

I talk. I speak to you of blues and greens,
temptations, lizards, tepid breezes,
and of fatigue and fondness, of wonting
and warning, and wherever you like I'll call to you

and fall to you. A song stretched
to the very temples of winter –
a sharp whistle and the sound of the sea: my head.

'I have nothing more for you each day'

I have nothing more for you each day
than dry flesh and strong wind,
having been or still being,
and the fulsome desire for the force of you,
the assurance that I know you and that your
soft hand brimming with homespun will find love.

I have no arm that's free, it only serves for me
to spot the things it does that you don't like.
I have a shaky bed in an open ditch,
eyes that are ripe, letters and certainties.

On this long train, deaf to us, with a heat that sears,
I walk to the back, give the Occupied sign a twist.
Wherever I am, I think of you, my love.
When there comes a knock, I say someone's in here.

'Let's sleep here just a little'

Let's sleep here just a little
let's make a blanket of olives
illuminate our fingers with truths
exchange breaths through the night
let's listen to lilac hearts
and give back the shadows
                              unite
within that grape of silence that gives us sight.

'Slowly watering the flowers of laughter'

Slowly watering the flowers of laughter,
I proceed from snowfall to snowfall and fire to fire,
turning northeast from Eden ever after,
across lands of stone and manure,
with small words to be found
in the pockets of my pants that I keep still cold
beyond the presence of the gods of hearth here gathered.

And I stick my hands deep into my neat
and clean corduroys to go on my old stroll,
walking straight and sparing, putting down
my feet nimbly.
                    I'm not on the prowl
for winds and colours; I'm Peter, Chuck,
common names, not proper ones, that I toll
in a voice dull and subdued, shortened, while I walk.

from *Written from Memory* (1973)

Vol de nuit

1.

I cling to your hand as though having a name,
as though having the bones and the fear of being a man.
In the night, those lights that devour me
are the closed eyes of this hunger.

I charm the city as with an oath,
or an exorcism, or meaningful hand gestures.
You breathe gently and shake me awake
from years of silence and drought.

When you don't speak, you speak, and you know
the words I say and don't say.
In those acts of home in which you warm me

are the discovered islands: and I proceed
on the voyage alone, on which you forget
me, love, your newborn friend.

2.

Graduated in law and solitude,
in the darkness, as the rain shines, I search for you.
It's true that you watch, and true that you speak.
That all of us have fears and pure waters.

To what goddesses do I owe you, if I owe you,
what awe is this, if there is indeed a reason for it?
How to search for you, then, if you are here,
or, if you're not, why do I want to possess you?
Which eyes and which night?
                          That one
on which you were here because you spoke my name.

On telling me your name springs are born
in another part of the day, one that's true.

And the islands are our journey to them,
they are mountains of silence and freedom
that we carry in our mouths and secretly
in our blind but cognizant fingers.

In the end, neither you nor I seek;
it's in the voyage itself that we possess.

'Night of the seventh night, when stars shining'

Night of the seventh night, when stars shining
were the light residing in our own hands:
not quite blind enough, seeing through feeling,
this route of fruit sublime and waves off-land,

Not quite blind enough, a mouth or two kept
navigating mad toward sleep inherent
in what was known, wished, shown and felt
to be lost, more perfect in aband'ment.

There were two of us, many arms had one,
struggling against the struggle, breathing tight
on a beach of fires and exhaustion

between the shriek of sea and birds in flight,
calm with rage, large yet few and far between.
The verb to give – night of the seventh night.

'Born you were where the horses sate their thirst'

Born you were where the horses sate their thirst,
where the rivers are turned back toward the wind
and these winds chase each other to be first
into the essence of your nourishment.

You came from where the night changes colour
so very slowly, to shades of cactus and yellow;
from where the open poppy substitutes for
the scream, the peace, and the waxen seal

of unblemished matter, out of the joy
of silence that is just now emerging
– like you, upon the periphery

yet at the centre, with the force of living
that long hour of the very first day
in the staunch humility of being.

'You, woman of the lake, are of the wind and forge'

You, woman of the lake, are of the wind and forge,
of moss and gentility and contradiction.
Wolfgang might have written a different water music
on your unbounded body, open to this hand.

The breath of things and the verses without measure,
patternless and weary, that I write here this afternoon,
clothe us, comprehend us, and immerse us
in yet one more tranquillity of that poor and fleeting time

in which from afar we receive that sack of agonies
made of cloth and padlock. Whatever the case,
with the flame with which you burn me you also illuminate me,
dear woman, my rain of countrysides, and more, my love.

'What green or yellow, what alteration'

What green or yellow, what alteration,
what abusive death, and maximum feeling,
what feeble and firm chance reaches me,
what fleeting fog and weeping of oblivion

that, if it rings, carries a light to the side,
where the sun existed through another monsoon,
what chalice more pregnant and more covered,
what fly, a dull and dwarf-like mark;

what slumbering flower for the night
far from any sea I have in my head,
from any wind that might cover you and give us shelter
along the road where nothing grows cool.

The day opens at its middle, love; and it hurts you
this tomorrow without yesterday that might be forgotten.

'I neither speak of words in themselves nor of chrysanthemums'

I neither speak of words in themselves nor of chrysanthemums,
but of all those hours noosed round the neck.
A true poem is when we are newly wed:
knowing how to remove both flesh and stone

at that cry between death and another death
that keeps us wakeful yet weary
until there comes the cut that slices us open
and removes from us our deepest wells and deserts.

And so, my love, what I give you,
a kiss kissed on a body limpid and lucid,
is more than the verse I speak to you, whether
alliterating, sharp, or subjunctive.

I'm stuck to everything, even against my will,
and it's the river which invents the verse, not
limited to seeing just my face in the mirror,
but you, beyond words, beside me.

from *Forty-Two Sonnets* (1973)

'My wife of parma violets and cities'

My wife of parma violets and cities
hidden behind wind and ovum,
out of which are born the hours and generations
of green youth, of insane greenness, preparation

for the infinite name in my hand's possession,
such water that is welcomed to your lips.
My nimble wife, standing on the foundation
of truth, landscape open to my touch,

I speak to you of potent but tranquil fluids
under the painful and flowing rivers
that bind together lines and dice,

of games yellowed and sickly,
neither ours nor small nor even games;
I say to you world, and we become aware of ourselves.

'Of autumns mild as a sun seen rising'

Of autumns mild as a sun seen rising
on tips of fingers that have turned to leaves,
I speak, grow silent and start dividing
between the light that holds me and picks you,

'tween sea and seeking love, nothing at all,
yet so much itself, perfect of being,
like a pine in wind and needles which fall.
Of autumns, I speak of seeds, harvesting.

And I see – you must see – what mists unfurled,
what anxious burrows under trembling feet,
what lowland limits between us curdled,
what wonder in many people foreseen.

Dry eyes you have, and yet your hands so wet,
and it's the future which rules the present.

'Love and lovemaking and making love grow'

Love and lovemaking and making love grow
in a place that's watching you, and neither
your eyes nor your hair that go on dripping
succeed in sealing my mouth and fingers,

squeezing a sap of joy, need so acute.
Behind slow mountains, a range of colour
unmade in a bed of white absolute
constructing the land where you will demur,

where you'll exist, risen into the cove
of coral and octopus, and then where
you will be standing with the light woven:
From under me to world above, of air,

comes your ground and your flesh begun hither
in hard earth, in between girl and mother.

'About your right leg I am divided'

About your right leg I am divided,
whether I'm more fond of it than the two,
or if both are a beach where I've freed
the crimson-hot centre of loving you –

– a beach, I would say, only because bruised
I return to it like a fire shipwrecked,
lost, but certain of being encountered,
inside unpredictable acts aimed at finding you

and of having you ever more fully when holding
something small which earlier was the sea;
and I pay fully my own price without myself fulfilling,

I'm reborn in your body and your gaze,
in you I see myself continuing on, without undoing
the core, the secret password, the having and giving.

'If it's from our hands the dawn releases us'

If it's from our hands the dawn releases us,
and the sun is born again beneath your skin:
I shelter your modest eyes and the quiet
immensity of your arm – and so it's that,

the strong but muddy helm of this life
that I want to give you and you give me,
that climbs the delicate mountains of the lost
pale flesh found at the foot of peace,

and if it waits, sparing and dissatisfied,
in the intense and fleeting and circumscribed world
that explains and creates and triumphs over the world made

of the shadows that we have fashioned. And if I inhabit
the smooth, soft dwellings of your breast,
then our love, my wife, is fixed and fated.

'Inside springtimes doubtful and impotent'

Inside springtimes doubtful and impotent
I enclose you, woman, in the mute frame
of the four winds hot and energy-spent
and on open road, a sharp whistle came.

From nothing does our love separate us,
living without root no more possible,
than luscious-leafed verdure lacking colour
when so worried with the futureable.

Hands given you, yours given me, giving
in this way to the earth and the gentle
cleanliness of our feet now walking

up the stairs, not flags, but tags and tables,
they are indistinct tokens or tollings
of a bell striking purity most fabled.

from *Now, To Be* (1975)

'*Go down slowly till you reach limbo*'

Go down slowly till you reach limbo,
give up your voice, your hands
and your marvellous memory,
look out of an old man's eyes at things,
keep sliding asunder, lacking meaning and direction.
Wanting not, seeing not, knowing not.
Dying is indeed the difficult thing.

'*The light that shines from stones, from the interior of stone*'

The light that shines from stones, from the interior of stone,
you gather it in, my wife, and then distribute it
so generously from the window of the world.
The salt of the sea slides across your tongue;
More in you is never too much.
Best of all, the flight of insects,
the nighttime rhythms of the movements of animals,
the key that unlocks that moment in when a
bird or cicada sings
– and the hand that commands all this plucks at the same time
the string that in you awakens
the dark eyes of each unique day.
Who are you saving with this mouth-to-mouth
resuscitation with the universe?

'A dog lingering at the stoop'

A dog lingering at the stoop
of a bitter doorway, of a door anywhere,
Shooting tenderness from my eyes.

A warm tongue that during times past opened
the depths of dark extremities,
now licks the rod that swats me
and, drooling, ceases not from loving the strike
– the one from the hand which has done its damage and disappeared.

Whimperings of happiness
at hearing the hand pass over me, while the wind cuts
in varying directions at the end of the street,
leaning my shaking head,
eyes angled and fixed on a small salvation.

Sitting on my own,
on my own upon the threshold,
on the rough mat – what joy.

from *The Circulatory System* (1978)

'Of snow I know nothing, nor of sun'

Of snow I know nothing, nor of sun,
of thousands of tranquillities awakened,
of the rising of your face behind your shoulders,
of the ardent hand, of the view from the balcony,
I know nothing.
I put down words as finished things:
it is only amongst them – as they turn, lightly,
their wheels of neither colour nor qualities –
that my science exists, though no longer mine,
or as much mine as yours or theirs,
air between fingers, juice of truth.

'Sorcerer lemon: painful purge'

Sorcerer lemon: painful purge
for that occult sourness
that our feet can never reach
and that (who knows?)
inundates the southland.
Gilded tow-rope
for the opposite meaning
– from the male and female centre
that quenches, nourishes, and explains to us.

You take your silence
from the ancient ship and extensive cavern
and the considered explosion
of compressed fire.

Shuttle, seesaw, pocket sun.

Sorcerer lemon:
both anchor and balloon.

'From out of moons and wheat fields I search a name'

From out of moons and wheat fields I search a name
until it is heard virulently spoken,
and something more than said or left behind
becomes, like myself, present and petrified;

from me, from you, I search for what is said
inside another sound so faithful and attentive
to the force of the tendril or the
girder that supports us;

from the sudden dusk-darkness I inhale the light,
intense, spilling across the paper
and passing on to the wood that leads it

to the earth, to the trunk, to the leaf, the flower, the honey,
the digestive tract, the wound, the emergent puss
of the day, naked, cruel.

So, in truth, there is no certain sum
of cause and effect, of breath and mouth:
each place is an open window

in the exterior walls of a castle, or a burrow, a warren,
or in flat fields of green or a deserted hand.
The immense night is a half-crazy mantle

that, covering with blue the fixed floor,
discovers vibrant veins, movement,
a shuttle of brief dreams from willing sleep,
through which everything passes without past.

In this way, from me, from you, it's not free
of light or a cricket or having been or spoken:
through time and dye there moves fast or slow
a continuing blowing, a hyphen of wind.

from *Horace and Coriace* (1981)

'Where were you when it struck four o'clock'

Where were you when it struck four o'clock,
and before that what were you, if you were?
Friend or enemy, may I speak to you now,
seated in front of me with your shoulders
stooped from the weight of your pen?
I will speak above your lowered head
and see beyond you, along the horizon,
your risks and your footsteps;
but I don't know where you went, nor if you were.
I look into your depths, under sun and rain,
gesticulating grandly or nodding lightly:
you speak old words,
from before four o'clock,
and there's nothing I know of you that you might tell me
out of that deaf head of yours.
I don't ask you for the truth,
what you think in the morning, or if you've already read Goethe;
or even if you've loved or love
mysteriously
a woman, a fish, a poppy flower.
I don't want that muteness of condolences
for myself, for you, or for the earth
that you and I walk upon – and eat.
I simply ask if you were,
who you were, and where you went
at four o'clock.

Could it be you don't have eyes? I don't see yours.
From farther and farther away
you shake your head, but perhaps it's a mistake.
I swear I don't understand you.
Friend, what's befallen you?

'It's eight days now, and I was eight years old'

It's eight days now, and I was eight years old
and everything was as real as coming out of the womb.
It's eight years now, and I was eight days old
and everything was equal in the coming and going.
Re-entering a dissolving dream is more back than forward
(coarse woollen cloth of song – what more could reveal me?),
and saying west is as about as useful
as splashing water on Lot's wife.
Better to point your finger at a spot on the map
and match your walk with the breeze:
to live with caverns of nothingness at your feet,
and die slowly, easing down into the earth.

'I, having neither father nor mother, do dishevelled'

I, having neither father nor mother, do dishevelled
declare, that I was not so very alarmed
when, being more sore than sickly,
they did not take me from my parents' home,
as I had neither them nor a house, nor am I
indeed a lad or a boy. I sent myself outside,
stupid, grey, and asinine,
and left for the fields where on danger I might dine.

'On remarking small tremblings'

On remarking small tremblings
or even the strongest jolt.
On remarking faintness
and the lights dimming out.
The morning that's born today lived yesterday
when spoken of later:
the blood is hot, but it's not fire.

'Now abandoned without any feeling'

Now abandoned without any feeling
of having been worthwhile or not,
with eyes open wider, accepting and loving,
strung like I don't know what animal,
with a gimpy leg like I don't know what man.
I look at A and B, and at you, still counting
on the position of the sea clearing that other beach,
so marginal but useful in another way,
so much the sea and marginal, undone but doing.
My dream home is not here, but where
I no longer dream of it. I live
standing, complete with what
another wind didn't have to give me,
and still more, with what I no longer have
nor aim to see again: the day is splendid,
death, as well, and the voice silent.
I cannot ask more than the gift of thirst.

from *Within Moments* (1984)

1

For the bee I have no solution
that the bee itself doesn't have:
honey and poison.

2

Do you see the bird descend precisely onto the leaf?
Might it not be the leaf itself which rises?

3

For the words that come down the river
I lay the net in which I lay myself,
and if I then fall asleep,
I awake
with eyes wide open.

4

So hard
that the feline pleasure
of true sleep
sweeps away fact, action, smile and thought
on one side only, on the mountain.

5

On the old man dies the arm
that has the hand inside its hand.

Orpheus at the counter was serving coffee
without being able to look at Euridice by her cash register.

The aim and the fear of changing while
the world changes without changing in any way.

The cloth flutters; does it remain something,
or is it form alone, female of the wind?

Going up from the tilled plain where he hoes the corn,
his callused hand lifted over his eyes,
he says: the sky is clear.

If twenty-four is even, then it is
only so in relation to forty-two.

The neck of the swan, they say,
provokes envy in women.
Swan, who taught you such things?

12

How much of a message passes,
trembling and swift,
through the croaking frog.

13

With nothing I fall in love unless it's
the palace in which I do not live
and that I would not want.

14

The luminous daughter of Autumn
was born at the end of an afternoon,
was born out of nine months.

15

On the floor of the scaffold the foot of the man
reverses the positioning of the stilts.

16

Free of fear, the dead.
But free of courage, too.

17

The tear that falls at sunset
across the cheek,
in so doing can no longer be
dew or sweat.

18

The dexterous man who modelled the vase,
afterwards looks at his hands
empty of it.

19

It's not with staring eyes but with the exhausted body
that you see the tree, indomitable, grow.

20

Alongside the morning was born another morning
where your foot, simply by touching the ground,
fixes time.

21

Children play guessing games
equally as well as adults.

22

In the blue plaster of the roof there's a sky
that's perfect and unflappable, just right
for our not having wings.

23

Playing guitar is that man
with nails.
And to the taloned player,
what instrument will you give him?

24

René said: I exist
– and then thought of something else.

25

The tolling of assets, yours:
a bell and ears.

26

From the light wind
another wind escapes ahead:
do you think they might stop?

27

Snow White took a bite of the apple
and her stepmother shouted out to the backyard:
There's your vengeance, Adam Dwarf.

28

The drop of dew wilts more quickly
than the rose in which it rests.

29

The one who neither loves nor hates,
to prevent boiling, turns sour like milk.

30

Now it's summer:
Apollo has grown up and
returned home too late.

31

Beautiful is the poem that's washed ashore
already nibbled by fish.

32

Along the slow miles that end the day
the feet hesitate more than the head.

33

Passive witness, the tear
that even in trickling down
with the eyes closed has
the unheard will of the poem.

34

It's the back of the gazelles, so desired,
that flees ever farther through the trees:
and ceases to exist.

35

Head in hand, tell me, Judith,
if each and every hair has been counted.

36

Stretch out your desire
far beyond your hand.
May distance excuse
what you don't have.

37

At the tank-rim the frog trembles with foreboding
but no prophecy does it make.

38

The round, gentle, rosy hills
in the breasts of a woman,
firm and smooth,
are the ones which the wind most respects.

39

Inherited truths
pay such high taxes
that they're better avoided.

40

Fluttering are the breasts of women
because they move about
more than the air.

41

I give myself to the peace of having been born yesterday
– today is too much, and more,
a mere appendix of history.

42

When the sun sinks over the world
what slumber will invite us
to hide ourselves?

43

The swift creature that climbs up the bark
of the wrinkled tree, what science
will it have, or have had,
of gravest gravity?

44

From the mouth emerged the kiss given
in a minute or a year
unspoken by the other mouth.

45

History without official papers, more real
than today's everyday life.

46

My eyes hesitate, and the seashore
exists without sentiment or significance,
without my looking or choosing.

47

The differences in light,
here and there, are united
by the land, my land and
this one.

Who knows more of lakes than we
who know the sea?

49

A finger rests on the table – briefly.
It's no longer the same, this table.

50

In my garden or in this one here,
it's really a question of squirrels.

51

Winged life passes us right by;
not even in an airplane do we truly fly.

52

Just like that friar mentioned by that other friar,
We meditate three hundred years in the garden,
or at least until the banks open.

53

The girl eats her chicken voraciously,
and voraciously drinks her soda.
Voraciously tomorrow,
Voraciously.

54

T'morrow we're sure to make a truce,
right after I screw my brother.

55

Time is born with the birth of the sun.
And so time is born everyday.

56

Beside grapes
we are but a dusting of insecticide.

57

The request of the bride's hand was made:
he stuttering a bit
and the father in law's ashes falling on the floor.

58

A peach-fuzzed man asked for melon.

59

The insomniac peeks out
at the light of day and says:
fuck it.

60

There's no manner to do it, no manner at all,
because we have no manners.

61

I put up with what you tell me, Leo,
because a constellation allows me to do so.

62

The tender eyes of a girl's childhood,
Oh Freude, Oh Freud.

63

What's the difference, what,
between a painter
and a man eating codfish?

64

The sea pants in its ebb and flow
and the three herons knit under the awning.

65

For what reason, tell me, am I careful
making caresses in the air,
illuminated
like he who writes in the sand.

from *Delphus, Opus 12* (1987)

'In all the earth so intense'

In all the earth so intense
no child cries.
No matter how much I grow and speak
no one from here hears me.
And so I understand, or I feel,
that the absence of noise
is less than silence
and nothing can triumph over it;
it enfolds, soaks up, inflames,
a catalyst for explosions,
the sound that dares ever more,
and the nothing that turns everything around.
In a single voice now,
once dissonant,
here are those who speak: listen up,
he who no longer has ears.

'Breast, centre, knot: place'

Breast, centre, knot: place
of connection in which opposites
unite. Just like what
was conquered here.

Keeper of sheep, friend of flocks,
but also of wolves. Lord and slave.
He is the shaman, but also he who would
draw sweet arrows whizzing out of death.
Lover of women who do not want him
and of the young of pointless deaths.
Player of the lyre, receiver of the flute.
Conquering desire and with it
denial. Clear and muddy.
Origin of twists
in the straight lines
where he has written obliquely.

Place up high and down low,
wide and slender,
black and white,
place and no place,
lost hope found.

'It lies between the Phaedriades more placid'

It lies between the Phaedriades, more placid
than the sea, that has ceased its delving,
and on the plain the olive trees branch out
in the untouched breezes.
It lies crumbled to stone
yet in stone created,
solar shade of the world
without any possible division.
The dull green and silver,
the roar burned to ashes by silence,
all the disturbances patent
but quieted.
Here, or nothing.

from *After Seeing* (1995)

Anti-Dürer

You live with me. Lock
fingers with me.
You eat with me, sleep, cough,
feed my hunger and abundance,
hoist up your bones as if my flag,
so intimate, immediate, intrinsic,
pocket-ogre, cone from a pine tree
standing right beside destiny:
death.

The Navigators

for Maria Gabriel

When late in the afternoon they sailed
the light from inside superimposed itself
against the sharp sequin of another sun,
moving at a pace opaque and equal, enclosing
disquieted arms, and the surprise
wounded them only for having been forewarned.

Against the cold salt crushed under their feet
and the deepening darkness, against the somnolent
scraping sound of rope and wood,
against the pangs of hunger and the weak moans
of a greying homesick longing, against the solitude
without mirror, the insatiable gluttony, the fear

– against it all, in enmisted times long passed,
their so very youthful passion struggled,
and it was one of seeing, of seeing with eyes wide open,
until feeling in their fingertips,
the tiniest passage, fuller even
than the cragged mountains of home and abroad.

the crinkling of a candle, a slow-moving fish
or one suddenly rising, unfamiliar flowers,
purulent colours, vast and sparing space
for strident birds open
upon a grand new life,
and yet still misty,
not knowing whether from this or another dream.

from *The Pennant of Charon* (1997)

'I have neither major character faults'

I have neither major character faults
nor qualities of greatness.
So the boat goes along
light of dangerous ballast.

And yet I have fortunate moments,
fleeting memories, subtle loves,
bodily sensations more than feelings.
Could this be enough canvas for the sail,
enough for wind and even a dry oar for rowing?

'The automobiles sleep. In the disco'

The automobiles sleep. In the disco
the couples titillating each other are dead.
On reaching for the telephone Roy
withdraws. And doesn't hear. And doesn't speak.
The flowers are blind periscopes:
they, too, don't get along, it's said.
Though the elevators ascend and descend,
they don't pass below the floor, like
something that falls – the percussion
of a drum or a guttural gong.
The sky is blue, or grey, or another
colour, from forever until forever,
but nothing more. It's more than clear:
So what? And even the wind, my friends,
even the wind blows like someone swallowing
himself, like a syringe or a telescope,
but immured. And the sea

wears out the waves from beach to beach
with the only result being froth.
Between the moon and the sun an accord was reached
yet no chord was played. They fade away:
there are no angels.

'What has been done is equal to what is done'

What has been done is equal to what is done.
What we feel inside equal to what is lied.
To try, to like, all fallacious
artifice that chills even torrid.

Illusory is the mansion in which you live as
dead, just like that one in which you pass away
in life – just as there is no grammar that can hide
from the rounded pain which no one can defray

because there simply is no one. There's no one
because no one is absolutely nothing.
Neither good nor bad – and what consists of
nothing more than a preposition of causing pain?

Everything is swollen, because it neither comes nor goes.
Undone, the knot sees itself undone to dust.

'what lights await our being'

what lights await our being,
beyond the ascent,
beyond this life we're meant?

'What you don't know doesn't exist'

What you don't know doesn't exist.
When a victory of fire
or a deafening and unexpected torrent of water,
or a beating of wings, light and hardly felt,
turns your eyes to silent corners,
to ears that until then had given you
only unmoving happenstance and your scrimping birth,
when a murmur awakens doubt
in what you had constructed with certainty
and a veil that you were not aware of in your ignorance
of whether it would lift, and, even more, when
you are able to see the hand that unveiled
a landscape of nostrils, fingers, pupils,

it is then that you exist, and the world rises inside you
and in you falls away the cavern through which you were feeling
$\qquad\qquad\qquad\qquad\qquad\qquad\qquad\qquad$ your way.

Other twists and turns you'll make, waiting once again,
until one day, suddenly, in a ray of light,
you might understand, understanding
that you needed to know that you again exist
and that what exists you can never expect to know.

'What you don't know now, you will never'

What you don't know now, you will never
know. Nor will you even know
why we speak today more of all sorts of things
than we did in the past. And whether the afternoon
agonizes or the boat slides
through banks of flowers along the river – all that is just
the perfect truth of a single day
which has taught nothing.

'She doesn't exist — we exist in her'

She doesn't exist — we exist in her.
It's with embarrassment that I state this
(though I must say something since I feel
that it isn't my end that's over there,
but the beginning), like someone who feels
his bottom at the edge of the chair, who sliding
off drops down slowly to the ground: that's the journey,
that's the river — or her.

'Arriving at the end of the road, you see from afar'

Arriving at the end of the road, you see from afar
that the beginning of the road doesn't exist. What you see
is neither pavement nor house, nor even corner,
what you see is neither happy nor sad,
what you see overwhelms your very eyes
because what you see is vacant.

The reason you are able to arrive, some people find,
is that your weight is equal to what you left behind,
along that road up which you never climbed.

from *Unspeakable Memory* (2000)

'My death, I cannot give it to you'

My death, I cannot give it to you.
Of the rest, you've had everything –
the flowers, siestas, and dusk-darkness,
the disquiet of rent day,
the destiny of mothers and of hands,
and of the curious words which say absolutely nothing.
You've had it all – I hope it's made you happy.

Happy for having everything I am.
Happy for losing all I've ever known.

Only I can't give you what I will no longer be.
No, my death, I cannot give it to you.

from *Previously Unpublished Works*
(1965–1991)

It's Day

What wind swept us
and spoke to us slowly,
what life and in whose gut was opened?
The hours which passed
have already switched places
our time is now a river.
The eyes with which I saw
a sun deserted,
a sun emptied,
are windows,
sails unfurled
for travelling.
Another place...

From the blood which made us
we are born again thus.
We die without dying,
to depart we were coming,
and the life which had us was fleeing.
And the smoke which hid
the door certain of leaving
flew from our empty voice.
Singing now is green,
it's a just-built ship,
it's a crossing,
it's the bread-sound,
a hand opened
to smiling.
Another requesting...

What wind swept us,
what given was given thus,
what death and agony
was made into day?

Ode

Agenda, my revenge,
that subtle swiftness with which I forget
youthful ways
in these fading days.

For what do you avenge yourself against me,
unless it's that beyond the parties and the shopping
I'm a man who must earn my bread?
Agenda, you're good at lending

but you neither give nor sell,
dressing me in ties and vests,
caressing me, consoling me, defending me.
I hide myself under lock and key in bathrooms

and jot down in you words that I unlive
in the fleeting stream in which I feebly laugh.
And so I free myself through cunning escape: close cut.

Not One More Word

Not one more word. Not one
will I say in birth or breath to the empty ear.
There's another light, I know: they will not condemn me.
And under the astonished light which spreads over the sea,
quiet, belonging to the boat, pregnant I'm going to burst
dispersed in the wind – and then I shall whisper
the letters that neither I, nor you, will ever read.